understanding
rugby union

ISBN-13: 978-1-905540-09-9
ISBN-10: 1-905540-09-4

Author
Julia Hickey

Specialist Consultant
Simon Worsnop

With thanks to Glyn Sutcliffe (indexer)

Cover photo © Alan Edwards

Throughout this publication, the use of pronouns *he, she, him, her* and so on are interchangeable and intended to be inclusive of both male and female rugby union players.

Published by

Coachwise 1st4sport

Coachwise 1st4sport
Chelsea Close
Off Amberley Road
Armley
Leeds LS12 4HP
Tel: 0113-231 1310 Fax: 0113-231 9606
Email: enquiries@1st4sport.com
Website: www.1st4sport.com

Produced and designed by Coachwise Business Solutions, a brand of Coachwise Ltd.
If you wish to publish some material for your organisation, please contact us at
enquiries@coachwisesolutions.co.uk

If you are an author and wish to submit a manuscript for publication, please contact us at
enquiries@1st4sport.com

060047

Contents

Chapter 1   Getting the Most Out of *Understanding* Rugby Union   1

Chapter 2   Rugby and Rugby Union Through the Ages   3

Chapter 3   Getting Started   6

Chapter 4   The Basics   9

Chapter 5   The Ingredients of Rugby Union   16

Chapter 6   Following the Progress of a Match   24

Chapter 7   Phases of Play and Set Pieces   33

Chapter 8   Being Offside   41

Chapter 9   Fouls, Obstruction and Misconduct   45

Chapter 10   Finding Out More   49

Glossary   50

Answers   51

Bibliography   53

Index   54

Foreword

Understanding Rugby Union, like the game itself, is fun and has something for everyone. With key information on the history, culture and traditions of the game, the book is a good, fun read. The clear explanations of the laws and of the skills of play ensure that it is informative. The quizzes that test your knowledge of the game, the useful tips on diet and training and the profiles of leading players all contribute to make this a dynamic and proactive resource.

For me, rugby union is the ultimate game. How do I come to that conclusion? Simply, the game can be played and enjoyed by people of all shapes, sizes and ages and is a great, enjoyable way of getting and staying fit. The game encourages and develops skills, such as running, evasion, throwing, catching, jumping and pushing and, for the more robust players, tackling and scrummaging. Rugby union has many different playing formats where these skills can be applied, some of which include non-contact touch rugby and tag rugby, the fast-growing and popular beach rugby plus the seven-a-side, 10-a-side and 15-a-side games. Whether you are male or female, fast or slow, big or small, rugby union has something for everyone.

Understanding Rugby Union is a fantastic resource to get you going; the short, simple paragraphs and bullet points cover facts and the important issues thoroughly, allowing the reader to access key points of the game easily. So whether you are interested in finding out more about the game by just dipping in and out, or are looking for a good read, this book is a must-have.

Nigel Redman
RFU National Academy Coach

I started playing rugby at the age of 10, and I wish *Understanding Rugby Union* was around then. It would have enabled me to have fun and enjoy learning the skills while also understanding the main principles behind the game. It provides a comprehensive insight into the rules and theories of rugby union, making it an instant hit with all youngsters!

Rugby union, to me, is a passion and a game that encompasses all skills, such as catching, passing, kicking, tackling and running. It's not only these playing skills that make it such a great game, it's also the fantastic team spirit that exists among the players.

Having been a professional rugby union player for over 10 years, I have enjoyed everything about the game and that's why I believe it is the best sport in the world – one that *Understanding Rugby Union* describes in a nutshell. Enjoy!

Matt Perry
Member of the England, British Lions and Bath teams

Chapter 1

Getting the Most Out of *Understanding* Rugby Union

There are three possible ways of reading this book. Whichever way you choose, have fun and enjoy rugby union!

1 You can read the book from beginning to end.
Most chapters are divided into three parts:
- The first part of the chapter provides information that will help you understand rugby union, whether you want to watch or play the game.
- The second part is a **summary** of key information about the laws dealt with in that chapter.
- The final part provides **training** tasks to help you check whether you have understood the laws and information covered in the chapter.

2 You can read just a chapter or a section of the book that you think might be useful to you:
- Scan through the book and look for the information (represented by icons) that interests you most. Below is a key to the icons.

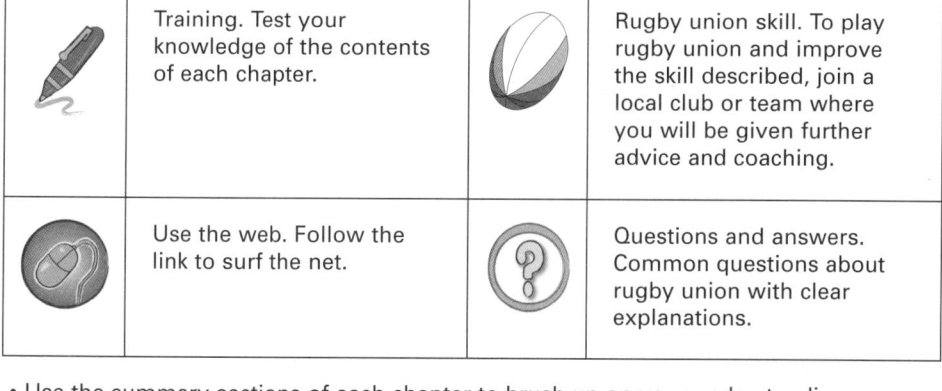

	Training. Test your knowledge of the contents of each chapter.		Rugby union skill. To play rugby union and improve the skill described, join a local club or team where you will be given further advice and coaching.
	Use the web. Follow the link to surf the net.		Questions and answers. Common questions about rugby union with clear explanations.

- Use the summary sections of each chapter to brush up on your understanding.
- Test your understanding by completing the training activities at the end of each chapter.

3 You can complete the following quiz to find out what aspects of the game you need to sharpen up on. Check the answers (you'll find these at the bottom of the page) to see how well you did and find out which chapters you should work on.

Quiz

1 What is 'tag rugby'?
- **a** A non-contact version of rugby union.
- **b** A ruse used by players if the line out is too short.
- **c** The Rugby World Cup mascot.

2 Which body is responsible for the rugby union laws and the principles behind the laws?
- **a** School
- **b** FIFA
- **c** The International Rugby Board

3 Can a team score a goal from a free kick?
- **a** Yes.
- **b** No – a goal can only be scored from a penalty kick.
- **c** Only if the free kick is taken within the 22-m line.

4 What is a 'mark'?
- **a** Something a teacher does to homework.
- **b** A type of catch that is followed by the catcher being given a free kick.
- **c** Grass and mud stains that you find on your shirt and shorts after playing rugby union on a wet pitch.

5 What is the difference between a 'ruck' and a 'maul'?
- **a** A 'ruck' is formed when the ball is on the ground and a 'maul' develops when the ball is being carried.
- **b** They are the same thing.
- **c** A 'ruck' involves lots of players mauling an opposition player who is trying to run with the ball.

6 Where is the offside line?
- **a** There is no actual line called the 'offside line'. Players need to know about the different phases and set pieces as well as open play, so that they can work out where an imaginary offside line would be. This is calculated in relation to the ball and other players taking part in play.
- **b** The line beneath the goal crossbar is the offside line.
- **c** The halfway line is the offside line for both the two teams.

7 When is a quick throw-in used to restart a game after the ball has gone into touch?
- **a** It is used if the team captain in possession of the ball decides that's what he wants to do.
- **b** It is used in the last half hour of the game so that both teams can enjoy as much open play as possible.
- **c** It is used by a player before a line-out has formed.

 See how well you do in the RFU's quiz at www.englandrugby.com/EnglandRugby/index.cfm?fuseaction=Juniors.Juniors_Detail&SectionId=467

or test your knowledge at www.englandrugby.com/EnglandRugby/index.cfm?fuseaction=Juniors.Juniors_Detail&SectionId=484

Quiz answers: 1, a (ch3 and ch4); **2**, c (ch2 and ch4); **3**, b (ch6); **4**, b (ch5 and ch6); **5**, a (ch7); **6**, a (ch5, ch6 and ch8); **7**, c (ch6).

Chapter 2

Rugby and Rugby Union Through the Ages

When, in 1823, William Webb Ellis picked up the ball and ran with it on the playing fields of Rugby, he was continuing a tradition that was already hundreds of years old.

'Football'

The Ancient Greeks and the Romans played ball games involving two teams. These historic games were not the same as rugby or football, but they had elements that modern players would recognise. By the Middle Ages, crowds of apprentices, who used inflated pig's bladders as balls, played games of 'football' in the streets and fields of Britain. There were very few rules and these games often turned into riots. It is not surprising that the authorities disliked these violent games and tried to outlaw them, though with little success.

The 18th and 19th centuries – 'football' becomes rugby union

'Football' continued much as before, until some enterprising teachers decided that sport would encourage team spirit, discipline and obedience in their unruly pupils. Public schools, such as Rugby, purchased land for playing fields, decided the rules and sent their pupils out to play 'football'. Unfortunately, everyone made up their own rules so, when two teams from different places met, there was very little chance of a problem-free match. Sometimes, games were played according to one set of rules in the first half of the game and another set in the second half.

Key dates in the 18th and 19th centuries

1750	Rugby School purchased some land and its pupils began to play 'football'.
1846	The first written set of rugby rules was published and circulated by pupils from Rugby School. There were four main rules that allowed running with the ball, hacking, tripping and holding. 'Hacking' meant that players were allowed to kick one another in the shins and some Rugby schoolboys wore metal toecaps in their 'football' boots especially for this.
1863	Eleven clubs met in London to agree 'football' rules. The Football Association (The FA) was born but, although rules based on Rugby's game were considered (handling the ball was to be allowed), kicking and tripping were forbidden. A number of clubs, as well as players from Rugby School, felt that this would destroy the character of the game and did not join The FA. Football and Rugby Union became totally separate games during the next decade – some organisations preferring to play by The FA's rules, while others continued to use Rugby School's rules.

1871 The Rugby Football Union (the RFU) was formed by 21 clubs. It was no longer legal to kick another player in the shins or trip them while they had the ball.

The first international match between England and Scotland was played in Edinburgh.

Scotland formed its own rugby union.

1879 The Irish and the Welsh rugby unions were formed.

1884 England, Ireland, Scotland and Wales all played against one another during the same season for the first time. This became known as the Four Nations Championship.

1885 Referees were given a whistle so they could control the game more efficiently.

1886 The first points system for scoring began to emerge in official games. The International Rugby Board (IRB) was founded with the responsibility of governing the Laws of Rugby.

1888 An unofficial British team toured Australia and New Zealand and a similar side visited South Africa in 1891. These touring teams evolved to form the British Lions (but they did not get their name until 1924 during another tour of South Africa).

1893–95 During the previous decades, rugby union remained amateur – no one was paid to play. However, a large number of team players, especially in northern clubs, were working men who lost wages whenever they played in matches held during working hours on a Saturday. Some of these clubs asked the RFU to allow them to pay the men who lost their wages. The RFU was determined that rugby union should remain amateur. They refused to allow clubs to pay men to make up for their 'broken time' at work. Northern clubs were angry about this decision, as it did not seem very fair that their players should lose money or that their teams should suffer because the men needed to work rather than play. Twenty clubs from Yorkshire, Lancashire and Cheshire resigned from the RFU.

Key dates in the 20th century

1910 A French team competed in the Four Nations Championship for the first time. By the 1920s, the Four Nations had become the Five Nations, but not for long; problems with administration procedures and the start of World War Two meant that it was only in 1947 that the Five Nations Championship became a regular event.

1983 The Rugby Football Union for Women (RFUW) was formed.

1987 The first Rugby World Cup tournament was held in New Zealand and Australia. New Zealand was the first team to win the Webb Ellis Cup, the trophy awarded to the World Cup winners. Since then, Australia, England and South Africa have all won.

The Web Ellis Cup

1995 The restrictions on benefits and payments to players contracted to rugby union were lifted. The game became professional.

1996 The Tri-Nations Tournament between Australia, New Zealand and South Africa was played for the first time.

1996 The 'sin bin' and a card system were introduced to deal with fouling players.

2000 Italy joined the Five Nations Championship and it became the Six Nations Championship.

2001 The International Rugby Player's Association (IRPA) was formed to promote the views of professional players.

Find out more facts about rugby at the RFU's website at www.england-rugby.com/EnglandRugby/index.cfm?fuseaction=Juniors.Juniors_Detail&SectionId=476 or take a tour through the museum of rugby history by visiting www.rfu.com/microsites/museum/index.cfm

Chapter 3

Getting Started

Rugby union is an action-packed game, filled with tension and teamwork – it is no wonder that so many people support their national team. Whether you are watching from a grandstand in the charged atmosphere of a world-famous stadium, sitting in front of a television screen, following the action, or just starting out on your own playing career, there are some basic rules you need to know in order to really enjoy the game.

©Alan Edwards

 How old do I have to be to play rugby?

There are players of every age involved with the game, from six years to 60. 'Tag rugby' is designed especially for players under the age of eight. This non-contact game is fun and develops some of the skills essential for you to be a successful rugby union player. 'Touch rugby' is great because it involves two teams of roughly equal numbers, a rugby ball and some space. In touch rugby, players with the ball must avoid being touched by a player from the opposing team if they wish to keep control of the ball, so it is largely evasive. Of course, it also develops those all-important kicking and passing skills. There are also other versions of the game, which are called 'mini contact rugby' and 'midi rugby'. Some variations in the laws help players to develop their skills and gradually move on to the contact elements of the game. The main thing is that these games are played in a safe environment under proper guidance so that everyone can enjoy themselves.

What sort of equipment do I need to buy if I want to start playing rugby?

It is important to have the correct footwear, so invest in a pair of rugby or football boots. Shin guards and a mouth

guard are personal items and should be purchased after seeking advice from your coach or from a specialist sports shop. It may be possible to borrow other safety equipment, such as headgear, from your club or team until you reach the stage where you need to buy your own. Make sure that the safety equipment you purchase is IRB-approved. If you join a club, your coach will give you further advice, such as making sure that you have a pair of gloves to grip a wet ball when training in wet weather.

I want to play rugby union. Do I need to eat a special diet and be very fit?

As well as natural skill and plenty of practice, rugby union players need to look after their health and fitness. First-class players need to have:

- strength
- flexibility
- speed
- agility
- coordination
- cardiovascular fitness (this means that

your heart and all the blood vessels work efficiently to pump oxygen around your body).

Players make sure they are consuming foods that suit their needs. Without a balanced and nutritional diet, the most talented player in the world will under-perform.

All professional players have dietary guidelines that they need to stick to in order to keep up their high-level performances. If players consume the wrong food and drink on a regular basis, they will not be able to train as hard or play for as long. Think about it: in a match, players need to compete for at least 80 minutes. This means that they need lots of carbohydrates to provide them with enough energy. Players also need to take care of their muscles – there is always the risk of injury – so consuming plenty of protein is also important.

Drink lots of fluid. Remember, fluid is lost through sweating during matches and training sessions. If your mouth feels dry and you are feeling hot, the chances are that you are dehydrated. It is important not to become dehydrated, as this will affect health and performance. Therefore, drinks – but not fizzy, sugary fluids – should be consumed before, during and after a training session or a match.

It is also important that players avoid muscle injury. You should always warm up before beginning a game. This prevents you straining muscles. If you do suffer an injury, it should be treated at once. Sports injuries can also be treated using a carefully adapted training regime that improves fitness gradually, over a period of time.

If you are just starting out on your rugby-playing career, it is important to eat and train sensibly. It would also be a good idea to join a local club or team where you will receive coaching playing skills, advice about what sort of exercise you should be doing and guidance on your diet.

What sort of things do I need to know if I want to start playing rugby union or watching the game?

You need to know the basics first: the pitch, the players' positions, the length of a match, who the match officials are and the scoring system. These are all explained in the Laws of the Game of Rugby Union.

These can be downloaded from www.irb.com/EN/Laws+and+Regulations/Laws/Laws.htm

Player profile
The youngest England player of the 20th century, **Jonny Wilkinson** began his rugby career as part of the under-18 squad touring Australia in 1997, after which he was signed by Newcastle Falcons and called to the England squad. He developed an impressive kicking record; he scored all 27 points in the 2000 game against South Africa in the second test and topped this in the 2001 Six Nations Championship in a match against Italy when he scored 35 points, setting a new Six Nations record. It is not surprising then that he was selected to fulfil his usual spot as fly half for the 2003 Rugby World Cup, where he set about scoring point after point, concluding with a nail-biting drop goal against Australia in Sydney and resulting in a historic English World Cup victory.

The spirit of the game

Remember that having the right attitude is also important. In fact, the spirit of the game is so important that the IRB has written the special Player's Charter, which sits alongside the Laws of the Game of Rugby Union to remind players that rugby union is about respect for the game and respect for everyone involved in the sport.

The Player's Charter reminds rugby union players that they are part of a team and have a responsibility to play to the best of their abilities. Here are some guidelines to help you develop your sportsmanship:

- Play by the laws of the game.
- Play as well as you can. This shows respect for your team, your opponents and yourself.
- Play to improve your skills.
- Treat all players as you would like to be treated.
- Applaud all good play, whether from your own team or your opponent's team.
- Remember that the referee is always right.

Finally, have fun! Enjoy rugby union.

 Find out more about the importance of the charter at www.rfu.com/microsites/handbooks/index.cfm?fuseaction=handbook.detail&storyid=8147

Summary

1 There are several different forms of rugby that can be played almost anywhere. There's even a special set of rules for people who want to play rugby on the beach. There are some variations in the under-15 and the under-19 games. The rules can be found on the IRB website.

2 The principles of rugby union laws are about team spirit, sportsmanship, skill, courage and mutual respect.

3 Play hard and play safely.

4 All you need to start learning how to kick and pass is a rugby ball but, to really develop those essential skills, it is important to join a club where you can get some coaching. You will also need a pair of football or rugby boots and all the necessary equipment to protect you, including shin guards, a mouth guard and headgear. Remember to look for products with IRB approval.

5 A healthy diet is important, whether or not you play rugby union. Try to eat five portions of fruit and vegetables a day. Avoid eating too much sweet or processed food, as these foods tend to contain lots of refined sugars, which are not very good for you.

6 If you want to become an all-time great player, join a local team or go on a rugby camp to get some more advice about diet and training.

7 Having fun and enjoying the game is an important part of rugby union.

 Training

A Keep a food diary for a week. Write down everything that you eat and drink. Check to see whether you are eating the right things to be a brilliant player. Make sure you are eating at least five portions of fruit and vegetables a day.

B Start to think about your level of fitness. It is important to build up your muscles and develop your fitness gradually or else you may injure yourself. The best way to get fit is to join a local team but here's a website that can help you to start finding out about what you need to do to get fit:

 http://news.bbc.co.uk/sport1/hi/health_and_fitness/default.stm

C Look at the information provided in Chapter 10 to help you find a local club.

Chapter 4
The Basics

A game of rugby union consists of two teams of 15 players each who are allowed to run, kick or pass the ball to one another in order to score points by getting the ball over the goal line. Players can run with or kick the ball forward but they must not pass the ball forwards. This means that teams have to be very mobile and must work together. The opposing team tries to stop them from reaching the goal line and making a touchdown inside the in-goal area of the pitch. Points are scored in four ways, by:

• scoring a try
• converting the try by kicking the ball between the rugby posts
• scoring a drop goal
• kicking a penalty to score a goal.

At the end of the game, the winners are the team with the greatest number of points.

All about...the rules

• There are 22 Laws of the Game of Rugby Union that ensure that the game is fair, exciting and safe to play.
• The Laws are the same whether players are amateur or professional.
• The Laws can be adapted (if there is an agreement) to meet the needs of different groups of players, tournaments or competitions.

Law 1 explains what a ground looks like, its size and what the different areas are called. It describes the boundaries and touchlines marked on the pitch, as well as detailing other features, such as the goal posts, crossbar and flags, that a ground needs before an organised match can take place.

Law 2 describes the shape, size, weight and construction of an official match ball.

Law 3 explains that a rugby union team is made up of 15 players. It also explains the process for making tactical substitutions or replacing injured players.

Law 4 explains what players should wear. It places emphasis on having the correct safety equipment.

Law 5 explains how long a match and the interval between the two halves of a match should be. It also explains that the referee must keep a note of time and allow stoppage time at the end of each half's play for injuries, substitutions and touch judge reports.

Law 6 explains how a referee is appointed, as well as his duties before, during and after a game. This law also explains the role of the two touch judges who assist the referee.

Law 7 explains the process for starting a game and describes the mode of play. This means it explains what the players can do with the ball and what they can do in the playing area to try to keep the ball or to remove it from their opponents.

Law 8 explains what an 'advantage' is and the situations where it is applied.

Law 9 explains the four different methods for scoring points.

Law 10 explains foul play and the penalties awarded to players for foul play. It also emphasises the respect that players should show for one another and the game.

Law 11 explains what is meant by 'offside' and 'on-side', as well as the penalties for being in an offside position.

Law 12 describes a 'knock-on'. The law explains that the consequences of a knock-on and throw-forward depend on whether the action was accidental or not. This law explains what decision the referee should make in both these cases, depending where in the area of play the knock-on or throw-forward occur.

Law 13 explains what a 'kick-off' is and where and how it should be taken. It also explains the circumstances in which a defending team should take a drop out (a type of drop kick) and how it should be taken.

Law 14 explains that, if the ball is on the ground or the player holding the ball goes to ground without being tackled, play must continue immediately. If a player deliberately makes a ball unplayable by lying on it, he is deliberately acting outside the spirit of the laws and a penalty kick will be awarded against the offending player's team.

Law 15 explains how a player in possession of the ball may be tackled and brought to the ground by one or more opponents. The player must be held and brought to the ground or else it is not a tackle. The player is only on the ground when one or both of his knees are touching the ground. If another player binds to the group, then a maul has formed so the rules for the tackle cannot be applied. This law also explains how a tackled player can carry on towards the goal line and, if he is able to get over the line, can score a try or make a touchdown.

Law 16 explains how a ruck is formed and how players must use their feet to try and gain possession of the ball. Penalty kicks are awarded against players who are deliberately unsporting during a ruck or whose behaviour endangers themselves or other players.

Law 17 defines 'mauls', explains how a maul is formed, how other players should join a maul and what offences can be committed during a maul and their consequent penalties. The law also explains how a maul should be finished, either with the ball being on the ground outside the maul or over the goal line. If a maul is unsuccessful, it should be followed by a scrum.

Law 18 explains that a 'mark' is when a player, who is on or behind his own 22-metre line, catches the ball cleanly from an opponent's kick (though a mark cannot be made from a kick-off). At the same time as catching the ball, the player must call, 'mark'. The law explains that the referee must award a free kick to the player who makes the catch, to be taken from the point where the catch was made.

Law 19 explains when and how throw-ins should be taken. It also explains when and how line-outs should be formed, as well as the options that may occur during a line-out. It also describes how the offside is determined during this process and the penalties that are applicable.

Law 20 explains what a 'scrum' is, how it should be formed and bound, the process for beginning and completing a scrum, what must happen when a scrum collapses and the penalties for committing a foul, being offside or being unsporting during a scrum.

Law 21 defines where penalties and free kicks should be awarded, how they should be taken and how the opposing team can respond to these types of kick. It also outlines how a goal can be scored from a penalty kick.

Law 22 explains the two ways in which the ball can be grounded in the in-goal area and the ways in which attacking players can score a try by grounding the ball in this area. It also explains that if a defending player grounds the ball in his own in-goal area or on a goalpost, it is called 'touching down'. This law also explains when the ball is dead and the penalties for committing a foul in this area.

All about...the different organisations involved in rugby union

The following organisations are sometimes called governing bodies. They are responsible for regulating, promoting and organising tournaments. They all use the same set of rugby union rules.

Table 1: The different organisations involved in rugby union

Organisation	Role	Website
The Rugby Football Union (RFU)	The governing body for rugby union in England.	www.rfu.com/index.htm
The Rugby Football Union for Women (RFUW)	The governing body for girls' and women's rugby union.	www.rfu.com/index.cfm/fuseaction /rfuhome.womens_home/ storytypeid/33
The Irish Rugby Football Union (IRFU)	The governing body for rugby union in Ireland.	www.irishrugby.ie
The Scottish Rugby Union (SRU)	The governing body for rugby union in Scotland.	www.scottishrugby.org
The Welsh Rugby Union (WRU)	The governing body for rugby union in Wales.	www.wru.co.uk
The International Rugby Board (IRB)	The IRB is the world governing and law-making body responsible for the Rugby World Cup.	www.irb.com

 Rugby union is a world game. Many countries have a tradition of rugby union or a developing rugby union culture. Visit www.scrum.com/links/worldrfu.asp to find links to these countries.

The RFUW

Women's rugby is a fast-growing sport. In addition to playing at grassroots level, women are taking the world by storm. Many famous tournaments, such as the Six Nations Championship and the World Cup, have a female equivalent.

Find out more about women's rugby at www.scrum.com/womens/default.asp and at www.rfu.com/index.cfm/fuseaction/rfuhome.womens_home/storytypeid/33

All about...the rugby union hierarchy

There are more than 1000 rugby union clubs playing in the country.

League tables, based on a points system, are drawn up to show how well each side is doing in relation to all the other sides of a similar standard and ability.

The Premiership contains the best teams in the country. Each team plays every other team in the Premiership twice during a season: once at home and once away. Points are awarded for winning, drawing, scoring four or more tries in a game and if the losing team's score is only seven or fewer points less than the winning team's score. At the end of the season, there is a play-off between the top four teams to decide who will play the team at the top of the Premiership league table. The winners of the final match at Twickenham take home the Premiership trophy, which has been sponsored by companies such as Zurich and, more recently, Guinness.

At the end of the season, the club with the fewest points may be relegated. The club at the top of the league below can be promoted into the Premiership, provided that the club meets a range of criteria (relating to stadium size, safety requirements, investment and community development).

Find out about Premiership news and clubs at www.rugbyclub.co.uk

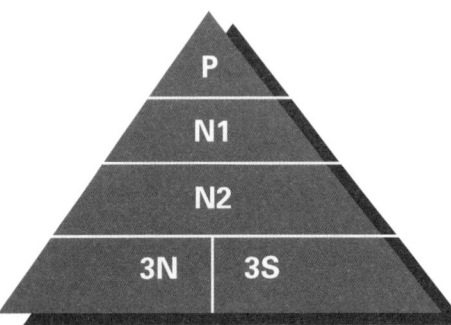

KEY

P = Premiership
N1 = National League One
N2 = National League 2
3N = National League 3 (North)
3S = National League 3 (South)

Some important competitions and trophies

England celebrate winning the 2003 Rugby World Cup

The **Rugby World Cup**, held every four years and won in 2003 by England, was introduced to the game in 1987. Since then, rugby union has gone from strength to strength. A number of places in the tournament are automatically filled by teams that reached the final stages of the previous tournament. Other teams must win their qualifying rounds, which are organised by continent into five pools. Winners and, in some cases, runners-up from these pools continue to the next round. The winners are decided in a variety of ways – sometimes, the winner is decided by a simple knock-out, while other teams reach the next round through a series of two-legged play-offs or by stages of round-robin competitions. Teams are pooled once more and the automatically qualifying teams seeded amongst them. Each of the teams in a pool play one another once. The top teams in each pool go on to the quarter-finals, with a hope of reaching the finals and winning the Webb Ellis Cup.

 Find out more about the Rugby World Cup at www.irb.com/Events

The **Six Nations Championship**, an annual event, is the longest-established international tournament in the world. The competing nations are England, France, Ireland, Italy, Scotland and Wales. In order to win a 'grand slam', a team must beat every other nation. **The Tri-Nations** series began in 1996 and is the southern hemisphere equivalent of the Six Nations. The competing teams are Australia, New Zealand and South Africa.

The All Blacks (New Zealand) celebrate their 2003 win

 Find out more about the Six Nations and follow the progress of your favourite team at www.6nations.net/splash.htm

The Calcutta Cup is the oldest international trophy, which is fiercely contested every year by England and Scotland as a separate competition within the Six Nations Championship.

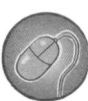 Find out more about some memorable Calcutta Cup matches by visiting www.rfu.com/index.cfm/ fuseaction/RFUHome.England_ Detail/StoryID/13215

The European Cup has had several formats and sponsors since its beginnings in 1996 and has powered forward to be a showcase for the best teams in Europe. Competing teams are divided into pools and each team in a pool plays the other teams in that pool. Points are awarded for a win, a draw, the number of tries scored and for losing by seven points or fewer. The winners from each pool and the best-placed runners-up continue into the next round of the tournament to compete for the coveted trophy. During the final stages of the tournament, matches can be decided through extra time and if this still fails to identify an outright winner, a place kick competition can be used to determine which team will hold aloft the Heineken Trophy. The European Cup is sometimes known as the Heineken Cup because of the sponsor's name. There is also a **European Challenge Cup**.

 Visit www.ercrugby.co.uk to find out more.

Countries with a culture of rugby union compete for their own national trophies. The **Currie Cup**, which is the oldest trophy of this kind, is fought over by South African rugby clubs. England has a long tradition of playing rugby for the sake of the game, rather than for any reward, but Premiership clubs do compete for the **Premiership** and there is also an annual tournament between English and Welsh clubs. The **Celtic League Championship** is a competition between Celtic clubs from Wales, Scotland and Ireland, who play one another at home and away to decide who will win the Celtic Cup.

 To find out more about the Celtic League, look at their website at www.celticleague.com/2_8.php

All about...famous rugby union grounds

Twickenham, home of English rugby, first opened its gates in 1909. The end of the 20th century saw a huge investment in it, making it one of the largest and most atmospheric sports venues in the world. **Murrayfield**, Edinburgh's iconic stadium, was officially opened in 1925 and saw the Scots win a match against England, completing victory over all five of the competing Five Nations that year. **Landsdowne Road** in Dublin is the oldest test stadium but Irish rugby needs a larger and more modern home for the 21st century if they are to compete as a world-class venue. **The Millennium Stadium** in Wales is just that: opened in 1999, it has already hosted some truly memorable matches. Finally, the **Stade de France**, just outside Paris, holds 80,000 spectators and is well used to presiding over action-filled finals.

 www.millenniumstadium.co.uk

©Action Images/Reuters

Player profile
Jonah Lomu, the 6 ft 5 in player who could run a 100 m in just under 11 seconds, established himself as a world figure during the 1995 World Cup. Here, playing for the New Zealand national team, the All Blacks, on the wing, he trampled over every team that the New Zealanders faced, scoring seven tries in five matches. Jonah repeated his world-dominating performance in 1999 but his international rugby career was brought to an abrupt halt due to serious illness. However, Jonah, who started playing for the All Blacks when he was just 19 years old, after representing his country in the national youth squad, has had a remarkable career, which has included winning a gold medal as part of the sevens team at the 1998 Commonwealth Games. Since receiving a kidney transplant in 2004, Jonah has renewed his passion for the game of rugby union, playing for New Zealand and for the Cardiff Blues. It is not surprising that he has received recognition from the IRPA for his contribution to the standing of the international game.

Summary

1 There are 22 laws that are designed to make rugby union an exciting, challenging and safe game to play.

2 Rugby union has traditionally been played for love of the game, rather than for trophies. However, there are some prestigious and historic trophies that are hotly contested.

3 The last decades of the 20th century saw the Rugby World Cup increasing the profile of rugby union around the world. There are now more people than ever watching and playing rugby union.

 Training

A Find out which club nearest to where you live plays Premiership rugby union. Use this link www.planet-rugby.com/Tournaments/Guinness_Premiership/Teams/index.shtml to see how well they perform.

B Which nation will you support in the Six Nations Championship? Find out more about the team you want to support and follow their progress through the competition.

C The Super 14 League is the southern hemisphere's equivalent of the Premiership. Find out in which countries the following clubs are based and list them in the appropriate column in the table below:

The clubs

The Blues, The Brumbies, The Bulls, The Cats, The Cheetahs, The Chiefs, The Crusaders, The Highlanders, The Hurricanes, NSW Waratahs, Queensland Reds, The Sharks, The Stormers and The Western Force.

The countries

Australia	New Zealand	South Africa

D There are some sides who tour the rugby-playing world, playing rugby union for the sake of the game. Find out more about these two legendary teams:

  i The British and Irish Lions

  ii The Barbarians (The Baa Baas).

Chapter 5

The Ingredients of Rugby Union

This chapter is about the essential components that are required for an official rugby union match. It also explores the way in which the game is controlled through the laws to ensure fair play.

All about...the ground

The laws call the area where the game is played 'the ground'. This is normally an area 100-m long and 69-m wide. The ground is divided into different zones by boundaries called 'goal lines' and 'touchlines'.

All about...the pitch

• Rugby pitches should be as near as possible to the dimensions shown on the diagram though it is not always possible for clubs to have in-goal areas that are 10-m wide.

• The solid lines, which include the dead-ball lines, the goal lines, the touch-in-goal lines and the touchlines, all mark boundaries of the field of play.

• The dead-ball lines and the touch-in-goal lines are outside the in-goal area. This is important. If a player tries to touch down to score a try on these lines, the try would not count.

• The goal lines are outside the field-of-play area but inside the in-goal area. This means that, if a player makes a touchdown on these lines, a try is scored.

• The touchlines on either side of the playing area are outside the field of play. If a ball goes over either of these lines, it is in-touch (which means that there needs to be a throw-in).

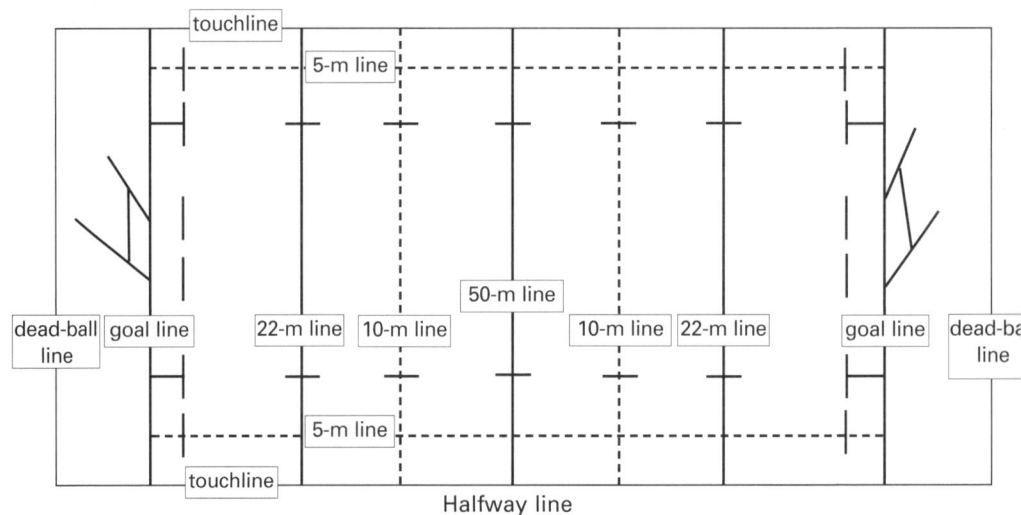

Figure 1: The rugby union pitch

- The halfway line and the two 22-m lines are solid but the rest of the distance lines are shown with dashed lines. These lines are used to mark zones for line-outs, to identify whether the drop kick that starts the game has gone at least 10 m and to decide how a scrum should be taken in order for there to be fair play.
- The pitch must be safe to play on at all times. Rugby should not be played on a hard surface, such as concrete, as this would be dangerous for the players.

All about...the goalposts

The goal is made from two upright posts, each of which must be taller than 3.4 m. A crossbar, 5.6 m long, is positioned between the two upright posts. The crossbar must be 3 m from the ground. Sometimes, padding is added to the bottom of the goalposts for the added protection of the players.

All about...the flag posts

- There are 14 flag posts.
- Each post must be 1.2 m tall or larger.
- Flags mark the halfway line and the 22-m lines. These flags are in the playing enclosure (outside the touchline).
- Flags are placed in the corners where important boundaries meet one another. One set of flags show the intersection of the goal and the touchlines. Another set mark the corners where the touch-in-goal lines meet the dead-ball lines.

All about...the ball

- The ball is oval.
- It is made of four panels.
- Its length from end to end must be between 28 and 30 cm.
- The circumference of the ball, measured along the line containing the two ends (the long bit), is between 74 and 77 cm.
- The circumference of the ball (the fat bit) is between 58 and 62 cm.
- The ball weighs between 410 and 440 g.

All about...the players

A team consists of 15 players, who wear numbered jerseys to show what position they are playing in. There are two distinct units of players on a team: the forward unit and the back unit. The forward unit is sometimes described as 'the pack'.

Player profile

Martin Corry first began playing rugby as a schoolboy in Tonbridge, before being signed by the Newcastle Falcons. Named Zurich Player of the Year in 2004/5, Martin has worked his way up from school rugby though to the Under-21 and the England A teams before appearing as part of the Lions squad in 2001. At 6 ft 5 ins, this number 8 stands head and shoulders above other players when he appears for England or the Leicester Tigers, both of whom he has skippered.

1. Loose-head prop
2. Hooker
3. Tight-head prop
4. Second row
5. Second row
6. Blindside flanker
7. Openside flanker
8. Number 8
9. Scrum half
10. Fly half
11. Left wing
12. Inside centre
13. Outside centre
14. Right wing
15. Full-back

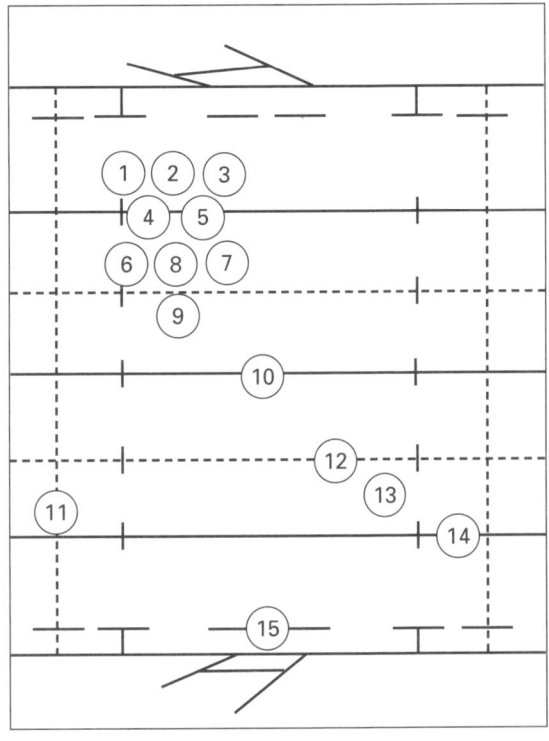

Figure 2: Positions on a rugby union field

It is very important that every player in the front row is trained and experienced so that the teams can play safely in scrums. Chapter 6 explains more about the responsibilities and positions of players.

What happens if a front-row player is sent off or needs to be replaced and there are no more suitably experienced players available to take his place?

If there are no more trained replacements available, the team must tell the referee who will then order uncontested scrums. An 'uncontested scrum' is a scrum the team throwing the ball must win. Neither team is allowed to push. This ensures a safe and enjoyable match for all those involved.

All about...substitutes and replacements

- A substitution occurs when, for tactical reasons, one player comes off the pitch and is replaced by another player from the same team.
- A replacement occurs when an injured player comes off the pitch and is replaced by another player.
- Teams may nominate up to seven players who can be substituted during international matches. Only two front-row players may be substituted at any one time, unless injury dictates otherwise. It is important that the substitutes are suitably trained to be in the front row.
- Names of the substitutes/replacement players must be given to the referee before the match. Players who have not been registered before the start of play are not allowed to take part in that game.
- Substitute/replacement players can only come on to the pitch if the referee allows them.
- Substitutions/replacements must be made when the ball is dead.

 If the referee sends someone off the pitch, can a substitute take the other player's place?

It depends why the referee has sent the player from the pitch. If a player has been sent off for foul play, he cannot be replaced with a substitute. The team has to continue the match a player down.

However, if the player has been sent from the pitch to be treated for an injury, he can be temporarily replaced by another player so that he can return to the game once the injury has been treated. The replacement becomes permanent if the injured player is out of the game for 15 minutes or more. A player who has been permanently replaced cannot return to the game.

 How does the referee decide if a player should be permanently replaced?

The referee receives advice from a doctor or officially recognised medics who are present at the match who can tell the referee how serious an injury is.

 Can replacement players be replaced?

If they're injured, yes. If they are sent off for foul play, no.

All about...the players' kit

Players must not wear anything that is dangerous to themselves or to other players, such as jewellery. Players should not wear boots with a single stud at the toe as this would be unsporting. All safety equipment must have an IRB approval mark.

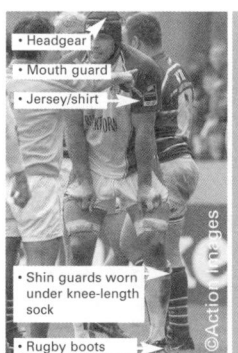

- Headgear
- Mouth guard
- Jersey/shirt
- Shin guards worn under knee-length sock
- Rugby boots

©Action Images

Players are inspected before the beginning of a match to check that they are properly dressed. If a player continues to wear an item he was told to remove, the referee can send the player off and award a penalty kick to the opposing team at the restart of play.

National teams wear strips with logos that are representative of the country to which they belong.

Choosing a pair of rugby boots

The main things to ensure when buying boots is comfort and, if they are studded, that they conform to IRB specifications (there should not be more than 21 mm between the sole of the boot and the tip of the stud). The external appearance may be appealing but if the boot is uncomfortable, you will not be at the top of your game. There is also a range of soles available, moving from the traditional screw-in studs to moulded blades, which are fine so long as they have no sharp edges. Some players favour blades as research suggests that they help with turning and acceleration. Others prefer the grip that the conventional metal stud offers.

How do I know if an item of equipment has IRB approval?
A full list of IRB-approved equipment is listed on their website. Visit www.irb.com/Laws/ Equipment to find out more.

All about...the referee

The referee makes sure the rugby union laws are followed during the match. Referees have the authority to take disciplinary action, from the moment they come on to the pitch until they leave, once the final whistle has been blown.

The referee:

- wears clothing that is distinguishable from the strips worn by the two opposing teams
- checks the players to make sure that their kit – especially their boots – meet the approved safety standards
- tosses a coin before the match to decide who gets the kick-off and which end each side will play from

- acts as timekeeper for the match – although there may be an official appointed to assist the referee as a timekeeper
- pauses the game if any laws are broken or any of the players are injured (if a doctor is required, the referee will signal as shown below).

- controls who comes on and off the field
- takes disciplinary action against players who are guilty of breaking the laws
- keeps the score
- works with the touch judges to decide issues of foul play
- during international matches, will work with the television match official (TMO) who watches a replay of any play where the referee is unsure of what happened – this means that a fair decision can be reached
- uses his whistle to start, stop and restart play and communicate significant events in the game such as a touchdown
- writes a report at the end of the match.

Signals

Communicating between officials and with the two teams is an essential part of being a good referee. Players and fans can also interpret these signals. The referee uses a whistle, two cards (yellow and red) and a number of hand signals to direct and inform players of his decisions. He will also speak to them – in many national and international matches, the referee wears a microphone so that television viewers can hear what he is saying to the players and other officials. There are a number of signals, some of which are illustrated throughout *Understanding Rugby Union* for you to keep an eye out for.

Referee profile Chris White began playing rugby for Cheltenham but made the switch into refereeing following a shoulder injury. He refereed his first international test match in 1998 and has gone from strength to strength ever since, refereeing the Heineken Cup final in Dublin between Toulouse and Perpignan in 2006.

All about...the touch judges

• There are two touch judges. There is one on each side of the ground.
• Each judge carries a flag to signal information to the referee.
• They signal whether a ball has gone out of play or not.
• They tell the referee the result of a kick at the goal. The touch judges stand next to the goalposts. If the ball goes over the crossbar and between the posts, the judge will signal by raising their flag that the goal has been successful (as illustrated on the right).
• They signal if the ball or the person holding the ball has gone into touch.

• They also show the referee where the ball was when it went into touch so that a throw-in can be taken from the correct spot.
• They help the referee to check that the throw-in is taken correctly.
• They help the referee to make sure the game is played fairly. They will signal any fouls that they see so that the referee can make a decision.

All about...the length of a match

• A match is 80 minutes' long.
• It is divided into two halves of 40 minutes each.
• There is a half-time interval of 10 minutes.
• Matches can last longer than 80 minutes because of allowances made for time lost during the game. Stoppage time can be added to a match by the referee (who keeps a record of minutes lost) to make up time lost because of substitutions, dealing with injured players, taking injured players off the pitch or the time taken for a touch judge to report foul play. The lost time is made up at the end of each half.
• If there is a scrum, line-out, mark, free kick or penalty kick to be completed as the time expires, the referee will allow the game to continue until the ball goes dead. It is also important to remember

that if a try has been scored, the referee will not finish the match until the conversion kick has been taken.
• If tournaments require an outright winner, matches are often allowed to go into extra time.

All about...winning

The aim of the game is to win! Teams win by scoring more points than their opponents within the time allowed. There are four methods of scoring points.

Table 2: The four methods of scoring points

Scoring method	Number of points scored	What the players have to do
A try.	Five points.	A player grounds the ball in the in-goal area. This means that the ball has to be on or over the opposing team's goal line.
A goal scored from converting a try.	Two points in addition to the five points scored with the try.	The ball must pass over the crossbar, between the two goalposts. The goal counts if the ball hits the posts so long as it goes over the bar.
A goal scored from a penalty kick.	Three points.	
A goal scored from a drop kick during open play.	Three points.	

What happens if the ball goes over the crossbar but is then blown back by the wind?
The goal counts.

What happens if a player should have scored a try but is prevented because a player from the other team commits a foul?
The referee will award a penalty try, worth five points, and will allow the conversion to be taken from underneath the goalposts.

Summary

1 Rugby union laws make safety a priority so that players can enjoy the game.

2 The 15 team members play hard as individuals but always work together as a team in open play, during set pieces (the scrum and line-out) and particular phases of the game (ruck and maul).

3 The referee and the two touch judges are responsible for making sure that there is fair play. They use the markings on the pitch to reach decisions about scrums, throw-ins and marks.

4 Scoring a try gives a team five points. Another two points can be scored if the try is converted. A try is converted if the ball is kicked over the crossbar of the goal. Points are also awarded for a penalty kick and for a drop kick that goes over the crossbar during open play.

5 In tournaments, where an outright winner is required, matches can go into extra time. Results can be decided based on the number of tries scored or by a penalty kick competition (this does not happen very often).

 Training

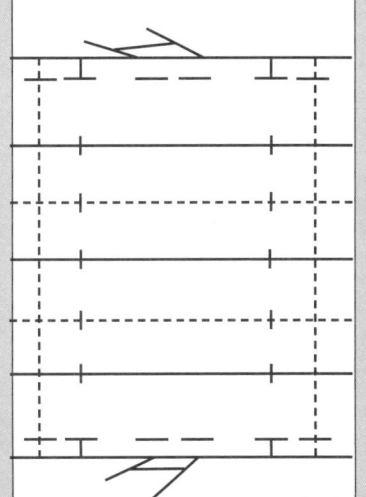

A On the right is a partially completed plan of a rugby union ground.

   i   Label all the different areas and boundary lines.

   ii   Identify the area that players must reach with the ball in order to touch down and score a try.

   iii   Add the dimensions of a pitch of international standard.

B Watch a rugby union match.

   i   Identify the different features on the ground and the dashed distance markings.

   ii   Keep a note of who scores points and how the points are scored.

C Health and safety is an important part of any rugby union match. List the ways outlined in this chapter that the laws make sure that the players enjoy a safe game.

D Explain the difference between a substitution and a replacement.

Chapter 6

Following the Progress of a Match

The role of the players during a match

It is important for players to behave as part of a team. This means that roles can change. Rugby union players need to be able to switch from attack to defence and back again during action-packed matches. The key thing is to play hard and to play fairly.

The forwards

The eight players who form the pack (all forwards) must try to gain the ball and then transfer it to the backs.

1 **The loose-head prop** stands to the left of the hooker and helps form part of the front row during a scrum. This means she needs to have lots of strength for that big push.
2 **The hooker** plays an important role in set pieces because it is her job to hook the ball back towards her team during a scrum and to throw the ball during line-outs. This means that she needs skill and accuracy as well as strength.
3 **The tight-head prop** stands on the other side of the hooker. During a scrum, when the two front rows are locked together, her head is between the heads of two opposition players. This is why it is called a 'tight-head' position. It also means that the props take most of the impact during scrums.
4 and 5 **Second row** players help push during a scrum and are usually the jumpers during line-outs.
6 and 7 **Blindside and openside flankers** are good at winning the ball from the opposition. This means that their tackling skills are well worth watching.

The **number 8** is responsible for retrieving the ball at the end of the scrum.

Player profile
Playing for the Northampton Saints, for England and the British and Irish Lions, **Steve Thompson** made his test debut against Scotland in 2002. At 6 ft 2 inch, he is definitely one of the largest hookers that England has ever seen and proved himself a valuable asset during the 2003 World Cup. He began his career as a schoolboy playing for Northampton before going into the Saints' apprenticeship scheme.

The backs

These seven players take the ball provided by the forwards and attempt to score tries.

9 **The scrum half** plays an important role in set pieces and needs to make quick decisions to gain ground and pass the ball.
10 **The fly half** usually organises the strategy used by the backs and is able to handle every aspect of the game.
11 and 14 **The wingers** need to know how to move quickly down the pitch and avoid the defence.
12 and 13 **The centres** need to play attacking and defending games. They must run, tackle and be able to pass the ball. Often, it is the centre who finds a way through the opposition's defence.
15 **The full-backs** often defend the area in front of the goal. This means that they need to be able to catch high balls and make decisive tackles in front of the

goal line, as well as providing weight during an attacking game.

Catching a high ball requires skill and nerve as well as plenty of practice. When you first begin to learn to catch high balls, get under the ball and make sure that your feet are solid on the ground and are set apart to help you balance. As you catch it, draw the ball into your body, as if you were cradling it. Many top-class players jump into the air to catch the ball. If you want to excel at catching high balls like this, join a local club where you will receive coaching and advice. Watch the way international players often turn side-on to give themselves protection from attacking players when catching, and notice the way that other players on the team give this player support.

Watch the video at http://news.bbc.co.uk/sport1 /hi/rugby_union/skills/default.stm to gain further advice.

©Action Images

Player profile

A full-back to be reckoned with, **Josh Lewsey** began playing as a schoolboy for the Amersham and Chiltern Club. By the time he was 18, he had been signed for the London Wasps but then moved to Bristol in order to complete his degree at Bristol University, after which he joined the army. Neither his education nor his army career could prevent him making his mark on global rugby, though, and it is little wonder that he was an important part of the 2003 World Cup-winning squad as well as a respected British Lions and, once again, London Wasps team member.

Starting the game

The process

The captains toss a coin. The winner chooses whether he wants to kick-off or which goal line his team wants to defend in the first half.

Each team must be in their own half of the pitch. The kicker's team must be behind the ball. The match is started by a drop kick from the middle of the halfway line.

The ball is kicked forward towards the opposing team's 10-m line. As soon as the ball has been kicked forwards, play begins.

The ball must reach the 10-m line, unless it is played by someone from the opposing team who has run forward and intercepted it once play has begun. If it does not reach the 10-m line and is not immediately intercepted by the opposing team, the ball is kicked again or a scrum is formed at the centre. The referee can also decide to play the advantage. This means that the referee thinks that if he stopped the match, it would be unfair to the opposing team, who have not committed an offence and who have gained an advantageous position.

The forwards on the kicker's team try to run down the pitch to intercept the ball. The opposing team's forwards also try to intercept the ball.

When the ball is caught, the player will try to run forward. The other forwards will try to bind round the player to protect him from the opposing team.

The opposing players will try to tackle the player with the ball and bring him to the ground so that he loses possession of the ball.

After the interval at half-time, the teams swap ends and the team who did not kick-off the first half takes the second-half kick-off.

What happens if the ball is kicked over the touchlines at kick-off?

If it goes directly out, the kicker's opponents choose a re-kick or a scrum back. If the ball has bounced before passing over the touchline, a line-out is called.

Open play

Players need to know tactics and strategies to get away from their opponents and into open space so that they can make a run for the goal line. Loops and dummies are common tactics. A loop occurs when a player makes a short pass to another teammate and then runs round the other side of the player to receive the ball back. It is important for a runner to be able to pass the ball to another teammate or to kick it forward so that he can retrieve it himself if he thinks he is about to be stopped. Remember, a player cannot be tackled unless he is holding the ball.

The aim for each team is to get the ball on or beyond their goal line in order to score a try.

• Players are allowed to run with the ball or kick the ball forward.
• Players are not allowed to pass the ball forward.
• A ball that is passed forward or which is accidentally thrown forward goes out of play. The game is restarted by a scrum.
• If the ball crosses the touchline, it has gone out of play. A line-out is used to restart play.

Forward passes and the knock-on

If a player throws or passes the ball forward, the referee will order a scrum, with the throw-in going to the other team, provided the referee thinks that the forward pass was unintentional. If the referee thinks the forward pass was deliberate, he will give the other team a penalty kick.

Top tip: If the ball drops to the ground but then bounces, it is not deemed a forward pass.

A knock-on is where the ball carrier loses hold of the ball or the player is trying to catch the ball, knocks it with his hand or arm and it goes forward.

Top tip: If the player can catch the ball before it touches the ground or another player, it is not classed as a knock-on.

The referee orders a scrum if he thinks a player has unintentionally knocked the ball on. The opposing team gets the throw-in. If the referee thinks the knock-on was intentional, he will award a penalty kick to the other team.

If the referee thinks that the offending player may have prevented a try from being scored by his actions, he will award a penalty try to the other team.

Player profile
Shane Williams, the Osprey winger, is 5 ft 7 in of pure energy and has proved his ability since first making his international debut for Wales in 2000. He confirmed his worth in the 2003 World Cup and went on to score three tries in five appearances during Wales' grand slam run in 2005.

©Action Images

Mark

If a player is on or behind their 22-m line and makes a clean catch from an opponent's kick, if he calls, 'mark' as he makes the catch, he is allowed a free kick; the mark is what is called a 'fair catch'. The kick is taken from the place where the mark was made. Marks cannot be taken as a result of a catch directly from kick-off.

Tackles

- Only a player holding the ball can be tackled.
- The player with the ball can hand-off would-be tacklers by pushing at opponents with an open hand. A closed fist that makes contact with an opponent is a punch, which is unsporting. It is also a foul.
- The tackle is only successful if the player with the ball is brought to the ground and held by one or more players from the opposing team.
- A tackle is not successful if:
  - the player with the ball is not grounded and held
  - the player with the ball is lifted off his feet
  - the player with the ball is not held.
- If a player is tackled to the ground, the ball must be immediately released. Tackled players try to pass the ball or release the ball as near to their own teammates as possible. The important thing to remember is that the ball must not be passed or pushed forward.
- A player cannot lie on the ball to protect it. This is obstruction and is not allowed.
- The tacklers should let go of the runner and get up before they can make a play for the ball. If the tackler has not released the tackled player, the referee will signal as shown on the right.

The laws are concerned that rugby union should be played safely and enjoyably. Once a tackle has taken place, players should get to their feet as fast as possible. It is unfair and dangerous to try and tackle another player on the ground. It is also important for players to remember that they can try to gain possession of the ball from behind the tackled player and the tackler rather than coming at them from the side, as this is dangerous. Players must try to get the ball away from the area of the tackle as quickly as possible.

If a player is on the ground and has possession of the ball, provided he has not been tackled, he must get up, pass or let go of the ball. If the player gets up as soon as he hits the ground, the referee will play the advantage; otherwise, if the player lies on the ball and prevents the ball being played, the referee will award a penalty kick to the other team. This is because the laws are written with player safety and fairness in mind. The ball cannot be played by players on the ground, and standing players have to be careful in case they fall on or over a player on the ground. If they deliberately land on a player who is on the ground, a penalty kick will be awarded against them.

Top tip: If you are tackled near the goal line, try to keep moving forward or reach out with the ball to ground the ball on or over the goal line. The try will count so long as the touchdown is legal. Opposing players can try to slow your momentum, and they can try to take the ball from your hands but they must not kick the ball as this would be dangerous.

What exactly does 'brought to the ground' mean?
If the player has one or both knees on the ground or he is sitting on the ground, then he has been 'brought to the ground' or grounded.

When is a tackle not allowed?
If a player does not have the ball, no tackling is allowed. If the player with the ball is tackled and held by one opponent, the tackle can be prevented by another player from the ball carrier's team binding on to the ball carrier. This forms a maul.

What happens if a player does not behave as the laws require?
It depends how the laws have been broken. There are different penalties for the player, including admonishment, temporary suspension and being sent off. If a tackle is incorrect, the referee will award a penalty kick against the team who infringed the laws, unless he decides to play the advantage.

What should the referee do if she is not sure who broke the laws during a tackle?
The referee should signal for a scrum. The throw-in will go to the team who was moving forward with the ball before the tackle.

Penalty kicks and free kicks

- A goal can be scored from a penalty kick but not from a free kick.
- If a team breaks the laws, the other side is given a penalty kick or a free kick. These kicks are taken at the place where the infringement of the laws occurred.

Are there any exceptions to this?
Yes, if the penalty or free kick is within 5 m of the opponent's goal line, the kick is taken on the 5-m line but in line with where the infringement occurred. If the referee awards a kick because of obstruction, the attacking team has the choice of where the penalty kick is taken from (either where the kick first took place or where the ball lands). Players choose to take the penalty kick from the more advantageous position.

- Players who take free kicks or penalty kicks can use any type of legal kick, so long as they do not use their knee or their heel to kick the ball.
- The ball must be seen to travel. This means that the referee must be able to see the ball move from the player's hands, if it is a drop kick, or, if it is on the ground, it must leave the mark.
- A team can choose a scrum instead of a free kick or penalty kick.
- The kick must be taken without any delay.
- All the kicker's teammates must be behind the ball when the kick is taken. The opposing team must be 10 m away from where the penalty is being taken, in the direction of their own goal line or on the goal line, whichever is nearest. Opposing players cannot take part in the game until they have reached this point, even though the ball may have been kicked if the kick is a penalty kick. If the kick is a free kick, the opposing team must retreat to the same point as for a penalty kick. However, they can then charge towards the player taking the free kick as soon as the player begins to make his approach to kick the ball, in order to prevent the kick from being taken. If the opposing players make a charge and prevent a free kick from being taken, the referee will order a scrum.
- If the kicker wants to score a goal from a penalty kick, he must tell the referee what he is intending to do before the kick is taken.
- Players taking a penalty kick may also choose to kick the ball into touch. This results in a throw-in being taken from where the ball went into touch. (In open play, the ball can only be kicked directly into touch if it travels from behind one 22-m line. Elsewhere on the pitch, the ball must land in play before bouncing and going into touch.)
- Common penalties are offside, barging, holding on to the ball or obstruction.

More about scoring

Tries (scores five points)

A try is scored when the ball is carried onto or over the goal line and is touched down. Watch out for dramatic chases as the ball carrier makes a run for the line and a touchdown. A try can also be scored by a tackled player who is close enough to the goal line for his momentum to carry him forward or to reach with the ball to make a touchdown.

©Action Images

Tries can be scored during a scrum. This type of try is called a 'pushover try'. Sometimes a scrum is formed very close to the goal line. The aim for the side attacking is to push the ball over the goal line while it is still in the scrum. The forwards push the other team back over their own goal line. The ball that has been hooked back by the hooker or by the weight of the scrum pushing towards the goal line is kept near the number 8's feet.

Once the ball is over the try line, the number 8 or the scrum half will touch the ball down. A try is scored.

- Once a try has been scored, the team are allowed to 'convert' the try into a goal.
- A converted goal is worth two more points so the team will score seven points in total.

- The conversion kick is taken at a point that is in line with where the try was scored. It is up to the kicker how far from the goal line the kick is taken.
- The ball is set up for a place kick. This means that the kicker can place the ball on the ground, a tee, sand or on sawdust.
- From the time when the ball is placed on the ground ready to kick, the kicker has one minute to kick the ball.

Doesn't someone hold the ball for the kicker?

A placer can hold the ball in place if the kicker chooses. One of the reasons for this may be that the conditions might mean that the ball would fall over during the player's run-up. If this is the case, the player has to kick the ball from where it has fallen or try for a drop goal. If the ball falls before the player begins his run-up, the referee may allow it to be replaced.

Goals from penalty kicks (scores three points)

Penalty goals can be scored from penalty kicks. The player taking the penalty kick must let the referee know what he intends to do. Once the player has made it clear what he plans to do, the players from the opposing team must stand still with their hands by their sides until the ball has been kicked.

- The kick must be taken from where the offence occurred or on the line directly parallel to it.
- The kick should either be a place kick or a drop kick.

Even if the player has not stated that he intends to take a kick at the goal and the ball goes over the crossbar, the goal will stand.

Goal from a drop kick (scores three points)

- A player can try to score a goal during any point in open play.
- Players cannot use free kicks to try to score a goal. This means that once the kick has been taken, the players on the team cannot attempt a drop-goal until an opposing member of the team has touched the ball or the ball has gone dead.

Summary

1 Individuals on a team fill specialist roles but to be most successful, players have to be able to work together and be confident either to attack or defend.

2 Once the ball is in open play, the referee and the touch judges ensure that the game is fair and safe for both teams. Penalty kicks and free kicks are awarded where the law is infringed.

3 Teams try to advance the ball towards the goal line in order to touch down and score a try.

4 The ball is 'dead' when it has gone into touch or when it has gone into the in-goal area and been touched down by a defender. It is also considered 'dead' when the referee stops the game and when a player is preparing to take a conversion kick.

5 Defending players may touch the ball down in the in-goal area or kick a ball into touch in order to move the game in the opposite direction, down the pitch.

6 Players may use place-kicks or drop kicks to score a goal.

Training

A Identify members of your favourite national squad. Add in their name in the spaces provided on the diagram.

1. Loose-head prop _____
2. Hooker _____
3. Tight-head prop _____
4. Second row _____
5. Second row _____
6. Blindside flanker _____
7. Openside flanker _____
8. Number 8 _____
9. Scrum half _____
10. Fly half _____
11. Left wing _____
12. Inside centre _____
13. Outside centre _____
14. Right wing _____
15. Full-back _____

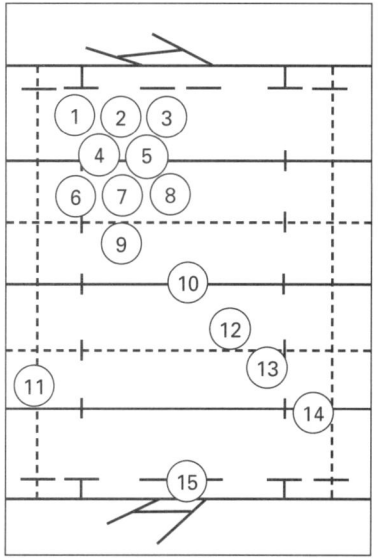

B i Look at the diagrams of the referee signalling. What penalty will result from the offences that the referee is signalling?

ii List in the box below some of the ways in which the laws of the game take safety in a tackle into consideration.

Training (continued)

C What type of kick is this player preparing to take? Find out how this kick should be taken and make notes in the box below.

©Action Images

D Note down the ways in which the referee and touch judges control the match in order to ensure fair play.

Chapter 7

Phases of Play and Set Pieces

The ruck and maul are phases of play that occur when the ball is in the playing area of the pitch but is no longer in open play. This means it is being contested for by players who have closed around it.

A ruck

The process

A ruck is formed when the ball is on the ground.

It starts when two players are in contact with one another and the ball is between them. Any player in a ruck must keep their head and shoulders no lower than their hips. They must only use their feet to gain the ball. It is wrong to pick up the ball during a ruck.

The heel of the back foot of the last player on either side of the ruck is where the offside line begins. Players not involved in the ruck should get out of the way of the ruck as soon as possible or else they will be considered offside.

Players can join the ruck so long as they join on their own team's side. They must also bind to the last player, not in front of him. To bind properly, a player must have at least one whole arm around their teammate.

A ruck is successfully completed when the ball leaves the ruck or it is pushed onto or over the goal line with the rucking players above it. If the ball leaves the ruck, it must not be returned.

If neither player gains possession of the ball, a scrum must be formed. The throw-in is given to the team that was moving forward before the ball became unplayable.

The laws of rugby union are about fair play and safe enjoyment of the game. This means that there will be penalties awarded against anyone playing dangerously. So, it is important to remember not to:

• jump on a ruck

• deliberately collapse it

• ruck players who are on the ground

• deliberately step on fallen players.

If a player breaks the law, they will normally be penalised with a penalty kick being awarded to the other team.

The referee illustrated is signalling that the players in the ruck failed to bind properly. It is important for rugby players to ensure that they do bind on correctly. Just putting a hand on a teammate does not count.

Does the referee always award a penalty kick?

A free kick is awarded for any technical offence at scrum or line-out but not during a ruck or a maul.

©Action Images

A maul

The process

A maul is formed when the ball is being carried.

↓

The player with the ball is tackled by a member of the opposing team.

↓

They both stay on their feet. Their heads and shoulders should be no lower than their hips as they push against one another.

↓

At least one of the ball carrier's teammates binds on to him. It is important to bind properly – the player's whole arm must tightly grasp the player, not just lay his hand on the player (see the photo above).

↓

Once a maul has formed, an offside area is created by two imaginary lines coming from the back of each team's last mauling player. These lines run the whole way across the pitch, from touchline to touchline. Players who come inside the area of the rectangle formed by the touchlines and the two imaginary offside lines will be offside unless they are coming to join the maul.

Players can join the maul so long as they join their team's maul behind the last man.

↓

The attacking team must be pushing towards the goal line. A maul is finished if it stops moving for more than five seconds.

↓

The maul is over when the ball or the player with the ball is on the ground. It also ends successfully when the ball is on the goal line. The ball is either in play again or a scrum is ordered.

↓

If a maul is unsuccessful because the maul is no longer moving, the ball is unplayable or the maul has collapsed – though not as the result of foul play – a scrum is ordered. The team that did not have the ball at the start of the maul will throw the ball in.

↓

If the maul moves into the in-goal area, a scrum from the 5-m line is ordered, with the throw-in being taken by the attacking team.

The referee is signalling that there is an unplayable ball in a maul.

The scrum

- The scrum is a set piece and is signalled by the referee as shown on your right.
- It is a way of restarting a game after minor infringements, such as a knock-on, an accidental offside or because a ruck or maul has not finished in a clear result.
- The referee will order a scrum if the ball, or the player carrying it, touches him and the referee believes that one of the teams has gained an advantage. If she thinks that play has not been affected, she will let play continue. The law is different in the in-goal area of the pitch.
- Referees may play the advantage if the other team swiftly gains control of the ball.

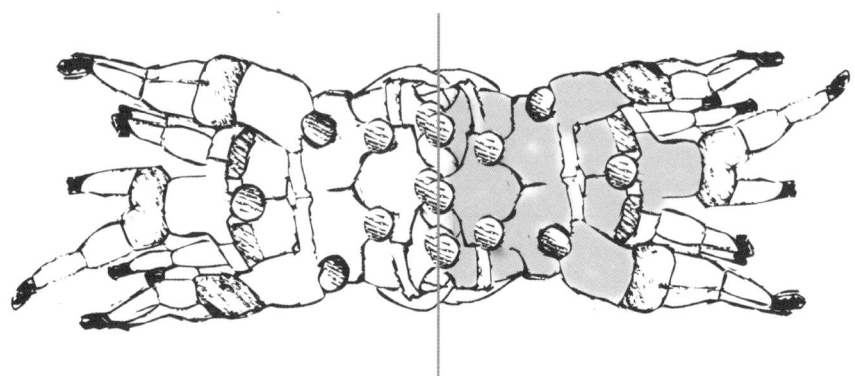

The process

The referee indicates the spot on the pitch where the scrum is to be formed. This is called a mark. A scrum cannot be formed in the in-goal area and must be at least 5 m from the goal line. The referee will signal to the players, as shown on the right, to form a scrum.

The scrum is formed by 16 players – the eight forwards from each side. The loose-head prop, the hooker and the tight-head prop bind together to form the front row. The two second rows, with the two flankers, bind behind them. The number 8 is at the back of the scrum formation. His back heel marks the start of the offside line.

Before the scrum starts, the two front lines must be facing one another not more than an arm's length apart. They then crouch and interlock. It is important that the players' heads are between the heads of their opponents and not next to one of a player from their own team. They only take this position when the referee tells them to engage. The coming together of the two front rows must not be a charge.

A tunnel is formed between the two front rows.

• • •

During this time, the backs get into position (being careful not to move offside) so that they are ready to move the ball towards the goal line if their forwards gain possession of the ball. They must not cross the offside line.

↓

The scrum half from the team that did not lose control of the ball throws the ball into the scrum. The ball is thrown straight along the middle of the tunnel formed beneath the two locked-together front rows.

↓

The two packs push against one another, trying to gain the ground over the ball so that they get possession. At the same time, each of the hookers is trying to hook the ball, with their feet, back behind them and into their own team's line of scrummagers.

↓

The scrum must move towards or away from the goal line. It must not turn like a wheel so that the line between the forwards is parallel with the touchlines. If this happens, the referee will stop the scrum and begin again.

↓

The ball comes out of the back of the scrum, in front of the number 8's feet.

↓

The ball can then be passed to the scrum half and, from there, passed to the backs. Alternatively, the number 8 will run forward with the ball. The aim for the number 8 is to get beyond the gain line. This is the place on the pitch where the ball was put into the scrum.

↓

If the ball does not come out of the scrum and the scrum is not moving, the referee will order another scrum.

A scrum is an exciting set piece that pits the two sets of forwards against one another. It is important to be competitive, to play hard and to play as part of a team. It is also important to play safely and to play sportingly. Remember:

- do not leave the scrum until the ball is out – players who stand up are offside
- do not handle the ball during the scrum
- do not deliberately collapse the scrum – this is dangerous and you will be cautioned or shown the red card
- do not deliberately fall or kneel in a scrum
- do not unbind
- do not lift both feet off the ground – your weight must be supported by at least one foot
- do not deliberately lift an opponent or force them upwards, out of the scrum.

The referee uses lots of signals to let the players know how successfully the scrum is being formed. The referee below on the left is signalling a wheeling scrum; the one on the right is signalling that the throw-in at scrum is not straight. Good communication between the two teams and the referee ensures that everyone can play a safe and enjoyable game.

 **What happens if the ball comes out of the other side of the tunnel when the scrum half throws it in?**

The scrum half will need to throw it in again. However, if a front-row player has touched the ball, the referee may apply the advantage law. If the referee believes a player was 'handed' the ball, he will signal as shown on the right.

 What penalties will the referee issue if players infringe the laws?

It depends upon the infringement. Free kicks are awarded where the process is not followed correctly. This would be the case if a team delayed in forming the scrum or the front rows did not interlock heads correctly. Penalty kicks are awarded when players are behaving in a deliberately dangerous or unsporting manner.

So, if one of the front rows unbound, it would be dangerous so a penalty kick would be awarded against her team.

 It is important for scrummagers to abide by the laws of the game and to be in the best position to push their opponents backwards. If two teams meet in a scrum, there is a good chance that the pack with the tighter formation and the best technique will win the ball, even if they are lighter than the other pack.

©Action Images

1 Keep your knees low and your feet wide (shoulder-width apart). This gives stability and potential pushing power.
2 Make sure your hips are below your shoulders.
3 Keep your chin forward. This will help make sure that you do not bend your back. It is important to remember that you are part of a unit. Someone could be pushing from behind you so a straight spine allows a more effective transfer of pushing energy and less likelihood of injury.
4 Get as low as possible.
5 Make sure you are tightly bound together. Your whole arm should be around a teammate – pull hard on jerseys and waistbands to help you grip.

Top tip: Rugby is fun to play but it is best learned and played in the supportive atmosphere of a local team where you will receive coaching and advice.

 Find out more about scrums from some famous rugby players at http://news.bbc.co.uk/sport1/hi/rugby_union/rules_and_equipment/default.stm

Player profile Lawrence Dallaglio joined the London Wasps in 1987. Six years later, he was part of the England Sevens World Cup-winning team. He made his debut for England in 1995 and, in addition to a stint as captain, he has represented his country regularly ever since and has taken an active part in many British Lions tours, as well as appearing as part of a Barbarians team. He has played in all the back-row positions but is best known as a number 8. He was named Lloyds TSB Six Nations Player of the Year in 2000. Although he retired from international rugby in 2004 due to successive injuries, he returned to the international scene in 2006.

Line-out

This is a method of restarting the game after the ball has gone into touch. Line-outs are not taken within 5 m of the goal lines.

The process

A touch judge or the referee points to the place where the ball passed over the touchline. This is where the throw-in will be taken from.

↓

The two sets of forwards line up in two parallel rows at this spot. There must be a metre between the two teams. Players must either be part of the line-out or 10 m behind the 'line of touch'. If players are not involved in the line-out and they are closer than 10 m, they are offside.

↓

Players who are in the line-out must not leave the formation until the line-out finishes.

↓

A player – usually the hooker – prepares to throw the ball.

↓

The receiver jumps into the air to try to gain possession of the ball. Often, the player will be supported in his jump by other teammates in the line-out. Once the player jumps, the other players are allowed to lift him higher in the air and hold him. It is illegal for the player who is jumping to use the players as support before he has made his jump. The player who makes the jump must try to catch the ball with both hands.

↓

Once the jumping player has made his jump and the ball has been won by one team or the other, the two teams must lower their jumping players to the ground.

The line-out may turn into a ruck or a maul. The line-out is only finished when all the feet of the players move away beyond the 'line of touch'.

Usually, line-outs finish when the ball or the ball carrier leaves the line-out. If the line-out becomes unplayable, the referee will order a scrum.

Summary

1 The ruck and the maul are phases within the game when the ball has gone out of open play in the playing area of the pitch while it is being contested.

2 A ruck begins when the ball is on the ground and three players contest it. A ruck normally starts with a tackle, whereas, in the maul, the tackled player stays on his feet.

3 A scrum is used to restart the game when the ball becomes unplayable or after specific infringements of the laws.

4 The 3–4–1 formation used by scrummagers is designed to help push the other team backwards and, at the same time, to try to gain control of the ball. There are other formations that teams can choose to use.

5 Scrummagers must abide by the rules to ensure safe play. The referee uses many different hand signals and gives lots of instructions to ensure that scrums are fair and safe.

6 Scrums can be used tactically. Defending players will ground the ball in their own in-goal area to prevent the attacking

team from scoring a try. After the ball has been grounded, the referee will order a scrum from the 5-m line.

7 Line-outs are used to restart the game when the ball has gone into touch. They cannot take place within 5 m of the goal lines. The aim is to win the ball from the throw-in.

8 Players not taking part in the throw-in must stand beyond the 10-m line or else they will be offside.

9 Phases and set pieces are designed to be fair and safe for everybody so that players can concentrate on skills, tactics and teamwork.

Training

A Look at this picture. Is it depicting a ruck or a maul?

B Explain your answer to question A.

C Watch a game of rugby union. Complete this tally chart to find out the number of rucks, mauls, scrums and line-outs that occurred in one match. Watch the signals that the referee uses to communicate what he wants the two teams to do.

Phase or set piece	Ruck	Maul	Scrum	Line-out
Number				

Chapter 8

Being Offside

If a player on a team has the ball, the other players on that team have to be behind the play of the ball (at the very least, behind their back foot) or else they are offside.

There are additional criteria for what is offside and what is on-side during set pieces of play, such as the scrum and the line-out.

Penalties for being offside

The penalties for being offside include:

- temporary suspension if the player is persistently offside or has deliberately stopped a try
- a penalty kick or a scrum with the ball being thrown in by the team who has been infringed against – the choice belongs to the captain of the team who has been infringed against
- a free kick being given to the opposing team for specific offside infringements.

The kick or scrum is awarded to the team from the place where the opposing player first went offside. The referee below is signalling for offside choice; either a penalty kick or a scrum can be taken.

Open play

- A player is offside if he is in front of a teammate who has the ball or who last played the ball.
- The player is only penalised if she then plays the ball, gets in the way of a player from the other team, does not move back on-side, moves within 10 m of the players on the opposing team who are waiting for the ball or approaches the place where the ball hits the ground.
- The referee will award a penalty kick from the spot where the offence occurred.

There are several ways of coming back on-side.

1 The player can move back behind the teammate who last had possession of the ball.
2 A teammate with possession of the ball can move in front of the offside player.
3 The player who last kicked or touched the ball runs in front of the player who was offside.
4 The actions of the opposing team may bring the player back on-side (eg an opposing player touches, kicks or passes the ball).

Top tip: If you know that you are in an offside position, get back on-side as fast as you can. If you remain offside you are loitering. Loitering is a form of obstruction.

 What happens if a player is offside, is taking no part in the game but then either gets hit by the ball or is touched by a teammate who does have possession of the ball? Providing the player was taking no active part in the game, he is judged to be accidentally offside. The referee will decide what to do depending on the outcome of the accidental contact. If the player's team has not benefited by the player being offside, the advantage will be played. If the referee thinks that the team with the offside player has gained a benefit, he will order a free kick or a scrum. The other side will throw the ball in.

 Are there any circumstances where a player has to stay offside?

Yes, if a player is offside when a set piece is formed, the player must stay in an offside position until the set piece has been completed. The player must not take an active part in the game as he is in an offside location. In order to get back on-side, the player must go back behind the offside line. This is in the interests of safety and fair play.

Offside during phases of the game and set pieces

A player is offside if she attempts to join any of these set pieces from her opponent's side:

Ruck or maul

• Players who are not taking part in the ruck or the maul should be behind the back foot of the last player who is taking part in the ruck or maul.
• If a player is not involved in play, they must be behind this line or they are offside.
• Players must not join the ruck or the maul in front of the last man in the ruck or maul. (If a player does, the referee will signal, as illustrated on the right.) The correct procedure is to join play behind the last man.

Scrum

• Players not involved in any of the set pieces must remain behind the back foot of the last player who forms the scrum. (If a player is offside at scrum, the referee will signal as shown on the right.) Only the forwards and the scrum halves are allowed into the scrum area.

• The scrum half with possession of the ball calculates offside as being the line of the ball as it is passed into the scrum. The opposing scrum half must wait for the ball to come out of the scrum before trying to gain possession of the ball.
• The players forming the scrum must stay bound until the ball leaves the scrum.

Line-out

- Only the forwards and the scrum halves are allowed to take part in the line-out. Players not involved with the lineout must be 10 m back from the line-out. If they come any closer, they are considered offside. (If a player is offside, the referee will signal as shown above.)
- There should be a 1-m gap between the opposing lines. If this gap narrows before the ball has touched the ground or been touched by a player, the players who come into the gap are offside. The only exception to this is if the players involved are jumping for the ball.

Top tip: Remember that a line-out has only been completed when one of the following four things happens:

- The ball is thrown beyond the 15-m line.
- The ball is passed back out of the line-out.
- The ball touches the ground.
- When the ball is caught and held, a maul is formed.

Summary

1 A player can be offside in open play but will not be penalised if they are taking no active part in the game.
2 Players must get on-side as soon as they realise their position or else they can be accused of loitering, which will be penalised as an obstruction.
3 A maximum of eight players per side is allowed to take part in the scrum. The front row must consist of specialist players. Other players must be the appropriate distance from the playing area or else they are offside.
4 Players not taking part in a ruck or a maul should be behind the offside line, which is an invisible line coming from the back foot of the last player in the formation.
5 If players decide they wish to join the ruck or the maul, they must join behind the last man or else they are offside.
6 If a player is not deliberately involved with the game but the ball or the player holding the ball touches him, he is accidentally offside.
7 The referee decides whether to play the advantage for offside offences or to halt the game and award a penalty kick to the opposing team.
8 Free kicks – not penalties – are awarded to the opposing team when a team closes the gap in a line-out too soon.

Training

A You are the referee. Decide whether the player is on-side or offside and what decision you would reach from these three choices.

a Offside but play the advantage

b On-side

c Offside and award a penalty kick to the other team.

i A player within 5 m of an opponent waiting for the ball is not taking part in the game and then retreats behind the ball carrier.

ii The scrum half feeding the ball into the scrum has his foot in front of the ball.

iii One of the forwards taking part in a line-out is less than half a metre from the opposing team's line-out before the throw-in.

iv One of the backs is closer than 10 m to a line-out that is being taken.

v A player is watching the progress of a maul, preparing to receive the ball. He is behind the last player on his side.

vi A player decides to join the maul. He joins from behind the last player on his team.

B Watch an international rugby match. Keep a note of the situations when the referee decides a player is offside and the penalties for infringing against the laws relating to being offside.

Chapter 9

Fouls, Obstruction and Misconduct

A touch judge signals that foul play has occured.

The aim of the rugby union laws are to make the game as fair as possible for everyone. They ensure that both teams have an equal chance of winning the game. They also prevent players from challenging their opponents in a way that is likely to be dangerous. Rugby union is about playing hard and playing fair.

Rugby union laws are very clear about what is fair and what is unfair. The laws also provide three ways, escalating in seriousness, for referees to remind players about the importance of fair play and to control the game so that everyone can enjoy a fair contest of skill and teamwork.

Admonishment

Referees talk with the players involved to tell them what they have done, that it is unfair and to remind them about the spirit of the game.

Temporary suspension

If an offence is more serious or if the referee has already admonished a player, the referee will show them a yellow card. This means that the player has been cautioned. He will be sent to the 'sin bin' to cool off.

Suspension

The player will be sent off the playing area after being shown a red card. He will not be allowed to take any further part in the game and his team will have to continue the game a man down.

The opposing team will be given a free or a penalty kick. Alternatively, the referee will play the advantage so that the game is fair to the team that has been fouled or obstructed.

Playing the advantage

An advantage is where the referee allows the play to continue after the rules have been broken or infringed. This is because, if the game were to be stopped, it would be even more unfair to the team who were offended against. The referee must decide whether the team who has been fouled has a tactical advantage or has gained enough ground for it to be considered an advantage. If the referee thinks neither of these things has happened, he will signal a penalty and bring the game back to the point where the infringement occurred.

Situations where the advantage will not be applied include:

- during a scrum, when the ball comes out of the tunnel without having been played
- when a scrum collapses
- when the scrum wheels – this means that the middle line of the scrum has moved through 90° so that it is no longer in line with the touchline but at right angles to it

• when a player is lifted into the air or forced up, out of a scrum.

What is the 'sin bin'?
The 'sin bin' is where players are sent to sit out part of the game for ten minutes after they have been shown a yellow card. Their team cannot bring on another player during this time. They must continue the game a man down until the temporary suspension has finished.

What happens if a player commits lots of different offences during a game?
A player who repeatedly commits offences will be punished with a yellow card; the opposing side will receive a penalty kick and then, if he commits another offence during the match, he may be removed from the game. Rugby union is about sportsmanship and there are penalties for players who are not prepared to play fairly.

Obstruction

It is unfair to deliberately get in the way of a player from the opposing team in order to prevent him from tackling your teammate who has the ball or to block the player to stop him getting to the ball first. This means that it is unfair to:

• charge or push the player (except shoulder to shoulder) to stop him
• shield a teammate who has the ball by running in front of him to block a member of the opposing team from making a tackle
• get in the way of an opposing team member in order to deliberately prevent him from playing the ball
• use teammates as a shield to prevent the opposing team members from tackling you when you are carrying the ball after a set piece, such as a scrum

• if a flanker, prevent the opposing scrum half from coming round the scrum by moving outwards during a scrum, even if he is still part of the scrum
• block the throw-in in a line-out. This means that the line-out players must be 5 m or more away from the touchline.

The referee will award the other side a penalty kick, which takes place where the obstruction occurred. The player who committed the offence will be shown a yellow card.

Unfair play

Rugby union is about sportsmanship. The referee will punish players who:

• deliberately waste time
• commit a foul to prevent a try from being scored
• retaliate against opposing players who are committing an offence – it is the referee's job to sort out the behaviour of the players
• behave in an unsporting way.

Dangerous play and misconduct

Players must not:

• hit, trip, stamp on or hack at members of the opposing team
• tackle players early, late or in any way that might be considered dangerous. This means that it is important not to tackle an opposing player above the shoulders or if his feet are off the ground (if a player does make a high tackle, the referee will signal as illustrated on the right)

- tackle an opponent without the ball unless it is part of the legal process of a set piece, such as a scrum
- deliberately cause a scrum, ruck or maul to collapse
- use illegal formations for their team – it is unsporting to use a 'flying wedge' or a 'cavalry charge'.

The referee will punish these offences with a penalty kick, unless he thinks that it is best to play the advantage. If the referee thinks that the offence has probably prevented a try from being scored, a penalty try will be awarded.

Where is the penalty kick taken from?

It depends. Usually, the penalty is taken from the place where the offence occurred. Unless it is within 5 m of the opposition's goal line, and then it is taken from the line.

A penalty at a line-out is taken 15 m from the touchline. A penalty not from a line-out and that occurs next to the touchline is taken 5 m from the touchline.

When are free kicks awarded?

If someone is accidentally offside, a free kick can be awarded to the other team. Incidents with line-outs, such as closing the gap between the two lines of players too soon or not having a straight line, will result in a free kick. The referee can award a free kick if players are not straight during a scrum or if a player in the scrum stands up.

Summary

1 The rugby union laws are about sportsmanship. So long as players respect one another and do not tackle one another in a way that is likely to be so dangerous as to cause injury, there is little chance of the referee being required to stop the match to admonish or suspend a player.

2 The touch judges will inform the referee if they see a foul taking place.

3 There are a variety of signals to show what kind of unfair play has occurred.

4 The referee will award a penalty kick, a penalty try or signal advantage, depending on the place where the foul, obstruction or misconduct occurred.

5 Penalties are most commonly awarded because players are offside.

6 The referee's decision is final.

Training

A Which of these signals might you see if the referee has seen unfair play?

i ☐

ii ☐

iii ☐

B Watch a rugby union match. For what offences are players sent to the sin bin?

C Decide whether the actions listed in the table below are offences or not.

Action	Yes/no
Tackling an opposing player around the neck.	
Tackling a player who has the ball in his hands.	
Lying on the ball to stop the other side from getting it.	
Pushing a tackler to one side using a hand-off.	

Chapter 10

Finding Out More

If you want to find out more about getting involved in rugby union, why not join a team? You could join a school team or your local club, where you will be able to play in a safe environment and receive coaching and advice about how to improve your skills.

 The RFU has a list of teams in your area and will be able to help you find a club. Visit www.england-rugby.com/EnglandRugby/index.cfm? fuseaction=Juniors. Juniors_Detail&SectionId=472 to find out more. Find out about becoming a referee or a touch judge at www.community-rugby.com

Top tip: Enjoy yourself. Rugby union is about having fun, being part of a team, having respect for the game and learning new skills. Who knows, perhaps you could be the next Jonny Wilkinson or Lawrence Dallaglio!

Glossary

Binding	'Binding on' is when players grip one another during set pieces, such as a scrum, to form a secure framework for the set piece to continue without collapsing.
Blind side	The opposite side of the field to where the three quarters line up for a scrum, ruck or maul.
Cavalry charge	An illegal attack, usually near the goal line, where attacking players form a line behind a player who has been awarded a free kick of some kind. The line of attackers charge forward, the kicker taps the ball to one of them. The defending players, who must be at least 10 m from the mark or behind their goal line (if that is nearer) until the kick is taken, are unable to move into position to tackle the player with the ball or defend their goal area. This is illegal.
Drawing	A player, with the ball, runs to try and force his opponents to tackle him.
Dropout	This is a method of restarting the game when the ball has gone into the in-goal area and a defending player has touched the ball down, making a 'dead' ball. The ball could also have gone over the dead-ball lines or touch-in-goal lines. The defending team takes the kick-off.
Drop kick	The ball is dropped from the kicker's hands. It bounces once. The player kicks it as it rebounds from the ground.
Dummy	To 'sell' someone a dummy is to pretend to do one thing but then do something else.
Flying wedge	An attacking formation where the ball carrier is protected by teammates in front and on either side. This is illegal.
Grubber	A ball that has been kicked and then bounces and rolls along the ground.
Onside	The opposite of offside. Players who are offside can be put on-side by their own teammates or their opponents. Players must be behind a teammate with the ball or who last touched the ball. They must not be within 10 m of an opposition player waiting to play the ball.
Peeling off	Line-out players peel off when they leave the line-out to catch the ball which has been passed back by a teammate.
Punt	If a player kicks the ball by dropping it and kicking it before it bounces on the ground, it is a punt. A goal cannot be scored from this type of kick.
Sevens	A version of rugby union played by seven players on each team.
Tunnel	The space between the two front rows in a scrum.

 Look at www.scrum.com/rugby_guide/default.asp for a full list of rugby union terms.

Answers

Chapter 4

C Australia: The Brumbies, NSW Waratahs, Queensland Reds and The Western Force. New Zealand: The Blues, The Chiefs, The Crusaders, The Highlanders and The Hurricanes. South Africa: The Bulls, The Cats, The Cheetahs, The Sharks and The Stormers.

Chapter 5

A See page 16 for the correct diagram.

D A **substitution** occurs when a player comes off the pitch and is replaced by another for tactical reasons.
A **replacement** happens when an injured player comes off the pitch and is replaced by another player.

Chapter 6

B i A penalty kick

C Place kick

D Referees and touch judges control the match by:
- using the markings on the pitch
- rewarding good and legal play
- penalising unlawful play with penalties to the opposing team
- sending players to the sin bin for bad and unsafe play.

Chapter 7

A Maul

B The ball is being carried.

Chapter 8

A i a, ii c, iii c, iv c, v b, vi b.

Chapter 9

A iii The referee is signalling a penalty kick – these are usually awarded to the team that has been fouled against.

Answers – Chapter 9 (continued)

c

Action	Yes/no
Tackling an opposing player around the neck.	Yes, this is dangerous.
Tackling a player who has the ball in his hands.	No, so long as the player has his feet on the ground and you do not tackle him above shoulder height.
Lying on the ball to stop the other side from getting it.	Yes, obstruction.
Pushing a tackler to one side using a hand-off.	No, the tackler is forced away by a push with an open hand. It is illegal to punch a would-be tackler.

Bibliography

Bath, Richard (ed) (2003) *The Complete Guide to Rugby Union*. London: Carleton. ISBN: 10987654321.

International Rugby Board (2005) *The Laws of the Game of Rugby Union*. London: IRB.

Past Times (2004) *A History of Rugby Union*. Green Oxford: Umbrella Publishing. ISBN: 095445619X.

Useful websites

www.bbc.co.uk
www.irb.com
www.irishrugby.ie
www.planet-rugby.com
www.rfu.com
www.scottishrugby.org
www.scrum.com
www.wru.co.uk

Index

Figures in **bold** refer to illustrations.

5-metre lines 16
10-metre lines 16, 17
22-metre lines 16, 17
50-metre line (halfway line) 16, 17
advantage, playing of 26, 45–6
advice 6, 7, 8, 49

backs 17, 24–5
ball, the 17
Barbarians, The 15
boots 6, 8, 19, 20
British and Irish Lions 15

Calcutta Cup, The 13
catching high balls 25
Celtic League and Cup 14
centres, the 18, 24, 31
clothing 19–20
conversions 29–30
Corry, Martin 18, **18**
crossbar 17
Currie Cup 14

Dallagio, Lawrence 39, **39**
dangerous play 46–7
dead-ball lines 16
dead-balls 30
dehydration 7, 8
diet 6–7, 8

Ellis, William Webb 3
  Webb Ellis Cup 5, **5**, 7, 13
English–Welsh club tournament 14
equipment 6, 8, 19–20
  approved by International Rugby Board
  (IRB) 6, 8, 19, 20
European Challenge Cup 14
European Cup, The (Heineken Cup) 13–14,
21

extra time 22
fair and unfair play 8, 46
fair catch (mark) 2, 27
field of play, the 16–17
fitness 6–7, 8
Five Nations Championship 4
flag posts 17
flankers 18, 24, 31
fly halves 18, 24, 31
food 6–7, 8
The Football Association (The FA) 3
footwear 6, 8
forwards 17, 18, 19, 24
forward passes
26, 27
fouls 45–8
Four Nations Championship 4
free kicks 28–9, 30, 34, 38, 41, 45, 47
front row forwards 18, 19
full-backs 18, 24–5, 31

gloves 6
goal lines 16
goalposts 17, **17**
goals (scoring)
  conversions 29–30
  from drop kicks 30
  from penalties 30
governing bodies 11–12
ground, the 16–17
grounds 14

halfway line (50 metre) 16, 17
headgear 6, 8, 19
health 6–7, 8
Heineken Cup (The European Cup) 13–14, 21
history of the game 3–5
hookers 18, 24, 31
hydration 7, 8

in-goal areas 16
injuries 7
  referees' signal for doctor 20, **20**
  and substitutions 19
International Rugby Board (IRB) 2, 4, 11
  approved equipment 6, 8, 19, 20
International Rugby Players' Association
(IRPA) 5
Irish Rugby Football Union (IRFU) 11

kick-off 25, 26
knock-on 27

Landsdowne Road Stadium, Dublin 14
Laws 8, 9–11, 15, 45
league organisation 12
Lewsey, Josh 25, **25**
line-outs 39–40
  and offside 43
Lions, British and Irish 15
lock forward 24
logos, national 20
loitering 41
Lomu, Jonah 14, **14**
loops 26
loose-head props 18, 24, 31

mark (fair catch) 2, 27
matches
  duration of 21–2
  progress of 25–30
mauls 2, 10, 28, 33, 34–5, 40
  and offside 42
midi-rugby 6
Millennium Stadium, Cardiff 14
mini-contact rugby 6
misconduct 45–8
mouth guard 6, 8, 19
Murrayfield Stadium, Edinburgh 14
muscle care 7

National Leagues 12
national logos 20

number 8s 18, 24, 31
nutrition 6–7, 8

object of the game 22
obstruction 41, 46
offside 2, 41–4
  and line-outs 43
  and mauls 42
  in open play 41
  and rucks 42
  and scrums 42
open play 26
organisations, governing 11–12

pack 17
penalty goals 30
penalty kicks 28–9, 30, 38, 41, 45, 47
phases of play 33–5, 40
pitch, the 16–17
place kicks 30, 32, **32**
players
  positions of 18, 31
  roles of 24
  suspension of 41
Players' Charter 8
playing area 16, 17
points scoring 9, 22, 29–30
Premiership 12, 15
  Cup competition 14
prop forwards 24

red cards 21, 37, 45
referees 20–1, 45–8
  and free-kicks 38
  and knock-ons 27
  and line-outs 39
  and mauls 35
  and offside 41, 42, 43, 44
  and penalty kicks 38
  and playing advantage 26, 45–6
  and releasing the ball 27
  and rucks 34
  and scrums 35, 36, 38

signals used by **20**, 20–1, **27, 31, 34, 35, 36, 38, 41, 42, 43, 46, 48**
and suspension 45, 46
and tackles 28
rucks 2, 33–4, 40
and offside 42
Rugby Football Union (RFU) 4, 11
Rugby Football Union Women (RFUW) 5, 11, 12
Rugby World Cup 5, 7, 13
Rugby League 4
Rugby School 3, 4
rules 8, 9–11, 15, 45

safety 19, 28, 31, 42
scoring 9, 22, 29–30
Scottish Rugby Union (SRU) 11
scrum halves 18, 24, 31
scrums 29, 35–8, 40, 41
and offside 42
uncontested 19
second row forwards 24, 31
sending off (permanent suspension) 45, 46
set pieces of play 35–40
shin guards 6, 8
'sin bin' see suspension: temporary ('sin bin')
Six Nations Championship 5, 7, 13, 15
spirit of the game 8
sportsmanship 8, 47
Stade de France Stadium, Paris 14
stadiums 14
stoppage time 21
substitutes 19
Super 14 League (southern hemisphere) 15
suspension
permanent (sending off) 45, 46
temporary ('sin bin') 45, 46
for offside offence 41

tackles 27–8
tag rugby 2, 6

teams 9, 17–19, 30
Thompson, Steve 24, **24**
throw-in 2
tight-head props 18, 24, 31
touch-in-goal lines 16
touch judges 21
and line-outs 39
signals used by **21, 45**
touch rugby 6
touchdowns 28
touchlines 16
training, physical 6–7, 8
Tri-Nations Tournament (southern hemisphere) 5, 13
try 29, 30
penalty 22, 27, 47
touchdowns 28, 30
Twickenham Stadium, London 14
uncontested scrums 19
unfair and fair play 8, 46

warming up 7
websites 2, 5, 8, 11, 12, 13, 14, 15, 20, 25, 39, 49, 50, 52
Webb Ellis Cup 5, **5**, 7, 13
Welsh–English club tournament 14
Welsh Rugby Union (WRU) 11
White, Chris 21
Wilkinson, Jonny 7, **7**
Williams, Shane 27, **27**
wingers 24
World Cup 5, 7, 11, 13
yellow cards 21, 45, 46